Gerald Dawe was born in Belfast in 1952. He has received various awards for his poetry, including the 1984 Macaulay Fellowship for Literature. He edited *The New Younger Irish Poets* (Blackstaff Press, 1991), and his most recent collection, *Sunday School*, was published by Gallery Press in 1991. He is founder-editor of *Krino*.

Aodán Mac Póilin was born in Belfast in 1948. He is actively involved in promoting the Irish language through his work as director of the ULTACH Trust; he is also a member of the Cultural Traditions Group and the Editorial Advisory Committee of *Causeway* magazine. He is the Irish-language editor of *Krino*.

GW00470251

Ruined Pages

SELECTED POEMS

PADRAIC FIACC

edited by
Gerald Dawe & Aodán Mac Póilin

THE
BLACKSTAFF
PRESS

BELFAST

First published in 1994 by
The Blackstaff Press Limited
3 Galway Park, Dundonald, Belfast BT16 0AN, Northern Ireland
with the assistance of
The Arts Council of Northern Ireland

Typeset by Paragon Typesetters, Queensferry, Clwyd
Printed in Ireland by ColourBooks Limited

A catalogue record for this book
is available from the British Library

ISBN 0–85640–529–9

Bells ring throughout the book
At the bottom of the lough

Gold running over the
Ruined page

from 'Tenth-century invasion'

We would like to express our deep gratitude to the poet Brendan Hamill, who, during 1973–4, shared with us his enthusiasm for the poetry of Padraic Fiacc, and introduced us to Patrick Joseph O'Connor.

G.D. and A. Mac P.

CONTENTS

INTRODUCTION

I

PADRAIC FIACC, now seventy, has been publishing for almost fifty years. The unmistakable shape and sound of his poems have found a lasting artistic echo in the personal and social traumas of his own life and times. That this poetry radically subverts what we often expect to see and hear in a poem is clear from the outset of *Ruined Pages*. The collection is intended to serve as an introduction to Fiacc's work – from the earliest surviving poems of the 1940s to those of the present – and also includes *Hell's Kitchen*, Fiacc's own account of the autobiographical and cultural sources of his writing.

The poetry of Padraic Fiacc departs from the Gaelic otherworld of myth and folklore before settling in the uncharted territory that is Belfast's violent history. It is a story, told with fantastic realism and melodramatic relish, which anticipates many of the most hotly debated issues of contemporary life and literature.

Fiacc's work is preoccupied with language as a physically despoiled body – the violated page; the exploded word-order. There has been much talk of late about the theme of inner exile and the use of dialect as a means of refurbishing the jaded artistic persona and poetic of contemporary literature in English. Here, too, Fiacc's work is central, for no figure of The Poet could be more isolated

1

and more aware of the fact than Fiacc himself, while his poems are obsessed with the actual word-ordering and depth-charged nuances of common speech.

Fiacc's ability to use idiomatic phrasing and cliché is a marvellous illustration of one of his poetry's main values. Similarly, the voice that in 'A slight hitch' describes the 'ghost/-faced boy-broadcaster' who breaks down, '(can you imagine, and him/"live" on the TV screen!)', is drawn against 'the usual cold, acid/and dignified way' of the 'NORTHERN IRELAND BRITISH/BROADCASTING CORPORATION'. This linguistic battle for authenticity, at the very heart of Fiacc's poetry, aligns him with the work of Tony Harrison and other 'Barbarian' poets of today. It is a verbal dexterity also paralleled by the imagery of his poetry, like the opening of 'More terrorists':

> The prayer book is putting on fat
> With *in memoriam* cards.
>
> The dead steal back
> Like snails on the draining board
>
> Caught after dark
> Out of their shells.

Throughout Fiacc's work the pervasive sense of childhood (of the poet's own childhood, of his daughter's and, in a bizarre way, of the entire city's) cuts up against the deadly inheritance of sectarian hatred and violence, 'crossing our stunted lives', as he writes in 'Glass grass'. It is the ordinary lives that are stripped of stability and forced instead to live with fear:

> She said she saw a man's head pass by
> The second-storey window.

2

'Och notatall granma
Or else he'd be an awful long
John Silver!'

Then the lamp was hurled
And geranium pot after geranium pot
Before whoever it was could
Find her a bed in the asylum from
Childhood to childhood, in a world
-womb to womb: to womb removed.

This comes from 'Dark night of the mill hag' and there are other similar portraits, like the Kafkaesque 'Dirty protest', which asks how life ever became so broken: 'Blown up, thrown down born alive.'

The intellectual legacy that shadows Fiacc's poetry draws upon a classic Catholic one, turned on its head and spliced with modernism, as Pascal, Mauriac, Baudelaire and Joyce coalesce in Fiacc's troubled imagination. There is, too, a wry, terse, almost despairing humour reminiscent of John Berryman, as in 'Intimate letter 1973':

Our Paris part of Belfast has
Decapitated lamp posts now. Our meeting
Place, the Book Shop, is a gaping
Black hole of charred timber.

Fiacc can also blend these poetic skills into a beautiful poignant lyric, such as 'Goodbye to Brigid/an *Agnus Dei*', with its opening evocation of Belfast offering up the unforgettable plea:

My little girl, my Lamb of God,
I'd like to set you free from
Bitch Belfast as we pass the armed

-to-the-teeth barracks and
Descend the road into the school
Grounds of broken windows from

A spate of car-bombs, but
Don't forgive me for not.

II

Padraic Fiacc's poetry traces his imagination's troubled and
broken course through the impounding claims of Irish his-
tory and mythology. Chronologically, *Ruined Pages* charts
Fiacc's engagement with both these forces – a process
marked by personal idealism, and then disillusionment
which, recoiling from any such 'logic' and withdrawing
from possibility itself, finally breaks down into the 'depths
of our dark/Secret being' ('Credo credo').

Up to and including 'First movement', the poems from
Fiacc's first published collection, *By the Black Stream*
(Dolmen Press, 1969), are written with a clear conception
of the Irish monastic style. Sharp syntactical inversions,
their bright colours, and sense of the world as a natural
wonder against which man is a sort of tragicomic intru-
sion: these traditional features conceal the stolen joy of
the poet in the world.

Yet these innocent perceptions seem to exist in spite of
the encroaching strain of the world, of experience threat-
ening to stain the poet's consciousness and it is here that
the jagged thrust of Fiacc's imagery takes over. 'Der
Bomben Poet' strangely anticipates Fiacc's poetic fate in
this regard. The more disharmonious nature is seen to be,

the more discordant and unpredictable the world, the more the poet tries to cast images in chaotic likeness, as in 'The ghost':

> Out of bull resentment
> Snores to the moon
> At black nightfall
>
> By my side a skull
> Hunted Dermot down:
>
> In all the land the lack
> Of what was whole . . .

Poems like 'Master clay', 'Lives of a student', 'Themes from a gloss' and 'Alive Alive O' are tuned in to each other. This complimentary process becomes disturbed and disjointed, however, at quite an early point, as in 'First movement'. Fiacc is obviously aware of the importance of this poem since he has brought it into two collections, marking points of hesitancy and anticipation of change. The poem is also notable for its accomplished simplicity and the characteristic contrasting of urban with natural imagery:

> I was born on such a morning
> Smelling of the Bone Yards
>
> The smoking chimneys over the slate roof tops
> The wayward storm birds.

But the following passage is particularly relevant here:

5

> And to the east where morning is, the sea
> And to the west where evening is, the sea
>
> Threatening with danger
>
> And it would always darken suddenly.

That sudden darkening and threatening with danger is the key perception which Fiacc makes of his disintegrating relationship with the world around him. 'First movement' demonstrates the characteristic style in which Fiacc's poems circle to the source of danger and threat; stunned by the sudden eruption of buried energies and forces that obliterate danger (which is immanent, an exposure to harm) with the deluge of reality. It is for this uncompromising recognition that Fiacc is best known, as he wryly says in 'Glass grass':

> My fellow poets call my poems 'cryptic, crude, dis -tasteful, brutal, savage, bitter . . .'

The tempestuous reputation that is all too often associated with Fiacc's poetry is deduced from the 'brutal, savage, bitter'. Yet such a reading is one-sided because it fails to account for the sources of Fiacc's poetry, or to describe the technical skills he brings to his writing.

The general impression given by Fiacc's work is one of entrapment: man is held in a painful stasis, pinned between the past and the future and, in this vision, images drawn from religion and impoverished social conditions coalesce. One of the most powerful physical images of this stasis can be found in 'Internee':

> It is not absolutely fair,
> It is not absolutely wrong,

> And it does not hurt
> To be jeered at
>
> When you are hanging
> Upside down,
>
> When hanging upside down hurts more.

As a cumulative condition, it is compounded of a range of imaginative experience. For instance, Fiacc's own experience of 'Ireland' as the conflict between an ideal world and terrible reality is a persistent theme in his poetry. In 'Icon' Ireland is the cause and effect of the individual's entrapment:

> Unholy mother Ireland banging
> On the wall in labour . . .
>
> We were born in her
>
> Screams to 'Get Out!'

But if Ireland is seen here as a mother giving birth, in 'Fire light' the life given is interpreted with existential despair:

> in this so strange
> 'So Be It Now' as if
>
> It never really were
> Or never will be
>
> Only always is . . .

Fiacc constantly stresses an enclosed, trapped world; one where 'We all run away from each other's/Particular hell' ('Intimate letter 1973') and the force that superintends the hell has an absolute stature in 'Our father':

>The evil thing being
>That which crushes us...

Fiacc rarely attempts to overcome the darkness but in 'The fall' he makes the gestures of rebellion:

>It's vengeance I want
>But vengeance on whom?

It is as if Fiacc refuses to acknowledge this life; our being is corrupt and his poetry speaks of the disintegrated ontology we have inherited with all its vast psychic (as much as social) injustice. But if Fiacc's work operates on this level in general, the poems deal with specific and identifiable onrushes of reality: the oppressive Military Machine, the deprived environment of a discarded working class, or the impact of mythology on everyday life, as in 'Elegy in "the Holy Land"':

>O dolly-Eurydice, my dark Ros
>-aleen dream
>
>>of bog on bog of bone
>-grounded cloud, Ireland, my dear
>
>Dragon seed pod...

Most poignantly this sense of failure resides in family life, where the contradiction between dream and reality is most acute, as in the imagery of 'Goodbye to our father':

>>I see your bone-naked
>Face scrutinising 'Injustices' still!
>
>Never bother! You have a hole to hide
>>in now...

If there is no release from the entrapment, if there

are no ways out, Fiacc can also see the black humour of being there. He does this through self-dramatisation and in the use of the aggressive understatements of Belfast vernacular speech.

It is with the urban landscape that Fiacc's poetry deals and in this he separates himself again from the general drift of Irish poetry. With its bases in rural landscapes – decayed, mythic or desolate – and its metaphoric wells sunk far from 'the damp down by the half-dried river/Slimy at night on the mud flats' ('Haemorrhage'), Irish poetry has tended to evade the city as imaginatively hostile or indifferent. In 'The black and the white' Fiacc strikes the exact note of city life, the hostility is embraced, the empty night-time streets, the loneliness, violence and loss:

> Sinking on iron streets, the bin-lid
> -shielded, battleship-grey-faced kids
>
> Shinny up the lamp post, cannot tear
> Themselves away, refuse to come in
>
> From the dying lost day . . .

It is not that city life is a contagion; in 'Our fathers' it is infected by industrial wastefulness:

> A grey cloud of pollution from Power
> Chimneys, mill house, laundries, cars . . .

When this environment is seen to be born of a corrupting past, the violent present spreads through every perception, affecting it with an inevitable meaning that imposes itself on our consciousness, like the remorseless rain in 'The wrong ones':

> The howl of the rain beating on the military tin
> Roof is like the tolling of a bell
> Tolling for a childhood more
> Murdering than murdered.

> I rise and stalk across the scarred with storm
> -erected daisies, night in the north, grass.

Throughout Fiacc's poetry, and in his past commentaries upon it and upon literature in general, there runs a deep hostility to the paraphernalia of art. Fiacc's Beckettian anti-art abandon caustically overthrows, so to speak, the pretentiousness of Art, while cauterising the poet's own unavoidable and reckless bonds with life. Fiacc's sense of himself as a poet is, accordingly, both mocking and tragic.

The often ugly parasitic relationship between literature and its immediate or historical world of suffering can, in Fiacc's book, lead to a neutralising of that suffering. Literature seems to stabilise the violence by drawing it into its own circuit of imaginative ordering. In the lived world the suffering continues to overwhelm. Such contradictions and ambiguities cannot be left out of the picture because they are part of the imaginative process: to excise them damages and destroys the terrible truthfulness that Fiacc's poetry struggles to articulate. For his poems dramatise the human effects of moral and psychological decay upon the lives of the ordinary people for whom, and of whom, he speaks. Time after time his poetry points to the erosion of human potential and the indictment is laid at the door of the political establishment.

No other poet writing in Ireland today has been so forthright and committed in saying the uncomfortable thing. Padraic Fiacc is the first of Belfast's poets to have imaginatively possessed, with such unremitting intensity, not only his own life, but the life of his profoundly troubled city as well. It is an extraordinary and disturbing achievement.

GERALD DAWE
1994

BIOGRAPHICAL OUTLINE

PATRICK JOSEPH O'CONNOR, the first surviving child of Bernard O'Connor and Annie Christina McGarry, was born on 15 April 1924 in Elizabeth Street in the lower Falls district of Belfast, and spent his early years in his grandparents' house in East Street in the Markets area. His father, who came from a family of well-off shopkeepers in County Cavan, worked as a barman in Belfast and was active in the IRA. During an anti-Catholic pogrom in 1920 his mother's family had been driven from their home in Lisburn, County Antrim, and their furniture – including the piano – burned. They settled in the Markets area in Belfast, where his mother worked in a fancy box factory. His grandfather never worked again.

His father emigrated to the United States in the late twenties, and was followed reluctantly in 1929 by his wife and three sons. The family settled in the Manhattan district of New York, where another son and daughter were born. For a short time they were relatively prosperous: his father had built up a grocery business and owned two shops, but the business failed, and he began to drink heavily. He eventually found a job in the New York subway and became a militant trade unionist. His wife hated America, and her longing for home intensified her sense of Irishness. She was very close to her eldest son, and read Yeats's poems to him.

He was educated at Commerce High School, and
Haaren High School, where he established a creative
workshop in which he produced a number of his own
plays. While still at school, he wrote a collection of im-
mature verse reflecting his experiences as an Irish Catholic
immigrant in America, which he called 'Innisfail Lost'.
The manuscript was submitted to Macmillan's, where it
was read by Padraic Colum, who asked to meet the
author, although he had been shocked by the explicitness
of the poems. Under Colum's influence the young poet
began to identify even more closely with Ireland: he
adopted the *nom de plume* Padraic Fiacc, and began
modelling his work on the technique and style of Gaelic
poetry, although much of his early work was written in
an identifiable American idiom.

In 1941 he began studying for the priesthood with the
Franciscans in St Joseph's Seraphic Seminary, Calicoon,
upstate New York. While there, he produced his verse-
play, 'Fire', and wrote a cycle of poems, 'River to God',
in memory of a fellow student who drowned. This collec-
tion was to have been published, but the seminary author-
ities decided it was 'morbid' and destroyed the plates. He
left St Joseph's, and continued his studies with the Irish
Capuchin Order at Holy Oak, Delaware.

In 1946 he abandoned his studies for the priesthood and
returned to Belfast, working briefly as a night porter in the
Union Hotel, Donegall Place. Seven of his poems were pub-
lished that year in the *Irish Bookman*, with a biographical
sketch by J.J. Campbell, which described him as a play-
wright and composer as well as a poet. He published fur-
ther poems and articles in the *Irish Bookman, Irish Times,
Poetry Ireland,* and *Rann,* and was the youngest poet to
appear in the American anthology, *New Irish Poets,* pub-
lished by Devin-Adair in 1948. In Belfast he began writing

14

fiction, and at least one novel, variously titled 'Night on Black Mountain' and 'The Bad Friend', was completed.

His mother died in 1950, and he returned to New York two years later to look after his young sister Mary. He had renounced his American citizenship while in Ireland, and had to re-emigrate. In New York he worked as a typist, and completed several other novels and plays. Early in 1956 a correspondence began with Nancy Wayne of Detroit, a painter who had read his work in *New Irish Poets*. They were married in August, in Belfast, and settled in Glengormley, a suburb to the north of the city. Their daughter Brigid was born in 1962.

Fiacc submitted a selection of his work for the 1957 AE Memorial Award, including excerpts from three novels, a complete play, and two collections of poetry, 'Woe to the Boy', and 'Haemorrhage'. The judges awarded him the prize, making particularly favourable comment on the poems in 'Woe to the Boy', the most Gaelic of the two collections. All but the poetry has now been lost or destroyed.

Fiacc had become friendly with the Belfast novelist and short story writer Michael McLaverty, who was as shocked by his novels as Colum had been by the early poems. For the next dozen years he continued to write and to publish in newspapers and literary magazines such as *Threshold*, the *Honest Ulsterman*, *Phoenix*, and the *Irish Press*'s 'New Irish Writing', but no volume of his poetry appeared until Dolmen Press published a selection of forty-one poems in *By the Black Stream* in 1969.

That same year the civil disturbances that had blighted his parents' lives in the twenties erupted again. They had a devastating effect on his personal life: his marriage fell apart and he himself suffered a nervous collapse. Later, in 1975, a close friend, Gerry McLaughlin, was murdered.

He edited a controversial collection of Troubles poems in 1974, *The Wearing of the Black,* and his writing developed a new, raw edge. The first volume of poems reacting to the violence, *Odour of Blood,* was favourably reviewed by John Hewitt in 1973. However, most critics appear to have been as disconcerted by Fiacc's late poetry as they were by his earlier Gaelic idiom. Several other collections have been published subsequently: *Nights in the Bad Place,* 1977; *The Selected Padraic Fiacc,* 1979; and *Missa Terribilis,* 1986. The Arts Council of Northern Ireland awarded him a bursary in 1976, and a major award in 1980. In 1981 he received the Poetry Ireland Award and was elected to Aosdána. Padraic Fiacc still lives in Belfast.

AODÁN MAC PÓILIN
1994

DER BOMBEN POET
Spring song 1941

Today is my birth
-day. I am seventeen.

My home town
Has just bin
Blown up:

Dead feet in dead faces,
Corpses still alight,
Students helping kids
And old people out of

Still burning houses.

I have nothing to write
Poems about.

This is my twentieth-century

Night-life.

RED MAN COUNTRY

For the first time
In a hundred years

The people here
Are counting their

Dead sons
            like
Children counting

Dandelions

     Calicoon, New York, 1943

THE NEW YORK NIGHT

Hailing a cab
I black out on tar
Am slapped back awake
By cop time nagging
'Do you know who you are?'

Stupid with justice and admiration
Youth old at Grand Central Station
Light pouring down from steel beams
In this subway still dares dreams?

Bags black porters carry to
A cab set me in mind of you
Bad companions of priggish vanity
Who set me in mind of me . . .

Will it ever be different?
Horizons fawned at of male or girl
For a tiny tip, a bob twirl
Up, flip down, crown or tails?

Tails when the gamble is spent
From cold Belfast to these hell-gales.

21

Emerging from this air-conditioned house
Of ill fame, I am this man, that mouse.

But what took the wind out of my sails?

THE OTHER MAN'S WOUND

In the communal shower after the drowning
We felt like Jews in Nazi Germany:

The water, flagellating down, took on
Something of the hostility in that
                                    dooms
-day for all who are born . . .

Soaping our sweat to goose pimples, we
Kept thinking about us, not him.

MASTER CLAY

On top of the mountain, the school,
                            a monastery . . .
I take the road up to the bells.
(The bells are a childhood memory!)

Monks are at prayer. Birds at laughter.
Bells peal in still blue air.

I am afraid of the wall of woods though
Afraid of the sea below, the shadow:
(Lest I fall!)
              'Come back down, you!'
Waves roar in blackening sky
'You will die for you carry your grave with you
And many's the worm!' I settle in my little cell.
It is not home: sea wind
Comes in cracks in my skull . . .
I climbed the whole way up the mountain to
An open wound rooted in the dead
In the ground is my very own
Clump of slime-green clay

Might not have ever been or
Having been is now but more!

LIVES OF A STUDENT

At the Feast of the Martyrdom
Of the Innocent
I knelt at the blood-red coverlet
Of the altar and dreamt
Sour morning crimson
Out of a long Lent

Phallic fern burn
Out of strong skull
Holes for eyes, poppies
And crocuses sprout
Out of the stale dry
Dust of empty soul.

I did not know I could
Not die and be done
With tulip fire in
Worm-raining sun
The roses of the flesh at noon
Leeched on the whittled bone

By virtue of the beautiful
Hungry greenfly
That every apple dawn's
Black bitter pit

Would arrow its light into
The eye of once
Young Sebastian.

THEME FROM A GLOSS

The mountain wall a roof
Higher than waves
Houses tall

Overhead over the book
Shadows
Of sea-wood dippers fall

Wing on wing on wing;
I cannot use my head at all

To copy psalms
With psalms
The water ousel sings . . .

Book in hand under
Wing-flowering oak
I learn better here
Than stuck at the school
Of auburn hair
Ablaze at her move.

I write.
       The cuckoo above

(By the way he can read)
Shits lime on the page
Cuckoos with me.

PRAYER

The monastery on the mountain
In the cloud is no haven
To take from what I should give
God. I seek no sanctuary from
The island not home
In demon childhood
Nor body by the worm
Bit to rag-worn bone.

Here is no more place to go
From being born
And in between birth more at death.

I pause hurled up on the jaws once were
A green shore of poison in the green
And gasp for breath

And fly fail climb fall back again
And pay the cost of time I waste and seek
Shelter against the wall
Like the fool Greek
Will bolt in separate directions after all!
O it is all wall and I am weak!

29

Wait until I am some old wreck
Sowed his wildest oat yet
Then I will want to climb your peak
And lie down on your steep brave bed
And count the rain of hailstones sweet
Hammer on hell from overhead
Free of chains of wings yank feet
Of clay would be safer rooted
In the enough nothing of the day
Chiselling to stone bone
A blur to thin line lands
I tightrope walk on
Any old which way

As with my feet as with my hands
As another one would pray.

ABANDONING STUDIES

I do not know
What salmon do

After they leave their young
In a cloud of milk

Or where they go
Or why lovers die

And I do not want to.

All the sages wrote
Their names in sand

Watched the mystery wash
'I do not understand'

With wave on wave
                    of wind.

I am content to be
brave as blind.

LEAVING THE MONASTERY

Goodbye giant pine.
Black branch give way
And each copper nut
Of star in the cloud.

I trek back down
Black blind blood
To the mill-tall town.

What did I learn up there?
What do I now know?

Boots go slip shod;

It is already
Blindly
Snowing.

THE SPRING FINDER

I am Rory's son, Conn's friend to God
And great Prince Conor on Connacht's sea
And Connacht's fog-drunken hilly lands
All bow low to me.

God makes the moon move when I move.
I am temple and king
And my soul is a tabernacle
To which angels sing.

My hands will bring forth of earth.
I and breaking waters are one.
Conor nourishes the ground
Being Rory's son.

THE BOY AND THE GEESE
for Brigid

The swans rise up with their wings in day
And they fly to the sky like the clouds away

Yet with all their beauty and grace and might
I would rather have geese for their less-smooth flight.

I would rather have geese for they're ugly like me
And because they are ugly, as ugly can be

I would rather have geese for their mystery.

JACKDAW
for John Hewitt

On Carnlough sand look up to sky
And let the waves come into beach.
The terrible great flying down of winds screech
That storm is good.

I am a jackdaw, and I am shrewd
And I have flown from beach to wood
And back again.

And I have nested in a tower
In hollow oaks and rabbit burrow
And in crevices of cliffs here.

So should you ask me, then,
I who have known flower,
I who have known furrow,
I who have known tear,

I who have built of sticks of straw
Of nest-lost and my own feather,
I who have tasted law
I who have tasted weather . . .

Should you ask me, should
I would say yes, and caw
That storm is good.

STORM BIRD

My comings and goings
Are the comings and goings of wind.

I am the word the wind mutters.
Pay me no mind.

Though I serve beauty and not mankind
The voice is the bird of a word
Wind gives wings to.

I am the blackbird
Of the ruined nest who sings

'All is beauty to the blind.'

AT AUTUMN BIRDS OF PASSAGE

Stay with us earth smell of air
And steam of dung.

Stay with us stint birds
Who make us dream
Of where you're from.

Bring back the bone-buried
Dog-eared old shoe of the heart
And out of it make

Out of a 'sow's lug'
A work here and there
Of ground-hollow art

And bridle, bridle the teeth
Of brutal night-life with

The bit of love.

OLD POET
for Padraic Colum

I

Strong as the seedling the clay
-reared winging bird, bald
But not bent head
The snow thawed on
A yellowing lead from time
(Rattled the lift he took
At night fornenst the park
As time as blood ran
Coming home in the dark)
Sings still the single word:

The workhouse and the road,
The turf bog, the poplar in Mullingar,
The furze bold as flesh,
The heather weather as blood,
The grain from the corn,
The trampling thresh of existence-limited feet,
The vision of futility,
As if it did not matter what
It is better not to be than born.

II

The pines stood up as guests about the Hundred and
                                        First Street Lake,
A table of frozen black glass.
He waved a hand up to the copper beech
To let the grey-faced student strolling with him
A twothree bit of say

Arguing about El Greco and de Valera
The eye more on the sparrow than the ear on his
                                        own word
Who strolled the streets of Dublin with James Joyce
And had, like the rest, a bit of a tiff with Yeats . . .

Under the iced branches of Central Park West
With a voice could be Daniel Corkery
Said what Yeats said what the best said
'Dig in the garden of Ireland, write of your own':

When we came to Ninety Sixth Street he
Flung eyes over the old roads
Of the midlands still looking home,
Blotted out a penthouse here to scan a hill there
Skimmed the snow on the grass as a boythrown stone
Skies the skin of water shyfully . . .

As seasons, passing, the rain
Left on the pavements where the pigeons are
The dead leaves of a summer sun . . .

III

Wind, a wren-wrought silk-for-nesting web
Closed over the havocked to ivory grass.
Smoked ravens with chimneys drifted
Filtered past hunched back silent cats of years
On a wash-line left hanging
Open gates: Unripened
Waiting, crude grain, raw

In the wood, still thriving from
Fermenting childhood's thinning comb
Of wine in time ripening
Truth, a beauty, and a good
Hive-sieve for man, the bee:

His wounds, birdmade, feet-pecked, scar-crowed,
Grin with beaks of panicking gold,
The shuddering wing gasping against the bar of the human
Hand touching the butterfly but not to death
With a green thumb forefinger clutch,
The touch of a mother of a woman

In a lifetime of peace, betrayed or told as a song
The moss winning left on the log,
He girds up his loins and laughs
At the buried bone dug up by the dog
At life, toothless toward nightfall.

NORTH MAN
for Michael McLaverty

Silent the river red in the snow.
In faltering twilight year after year
A lifting wind falls:
The red sun is down, the swans disappear.

Along the evening Lagan we
Walking the broken dream under the bent bough,
Stop to adhere to the birds,
Known and named, as if by Adam, by you,
Creating poetry without words
Building silence like a house.

I recall yourself and the birds
In tune with the sky gone down.

We walked with silence as if on a dream.
You spoke in the end as if on wind
But how far were your words flung like seed
Over stone

'Passionate and dense as the half-said thing'

Hungering like the teeth of the sea.

A CHILDHOOD FRIEND
for Colm

Too late into night not for the light
Of day to betray in flat relief
The pruck of smoke still hovering
Over the fry in the morning

Penniless with grief

Our paper wings, the chalked-up gone
Late at play, getting a drunk on
Man will rant and pray and lie down
And kick for not getting his fill

In the windy gap of the yawning hollow
Need for love in pools of blood:
Any child's big penny

Still flickering from each
Shadow seemed substantial: today
We hardly stand in one another's light

Time, weaving a rope of pee-the-beds
The fragile moment breaks the band

As we, our own paper boats

Alien to memory in a strange land
Need but a breath to drift to sea.

ALIVE ALIVE O

The altar boy from a Mass for the dead
Romps through the streets of the town
Lolls on brick-studded grass
Jumps up, bolts back down
With wild pup eyes . . .

This morning at twist of winter to spring
Small hands clutched a big brass cross
Followed the stern brow of the priest
Encircle the man in the box . . .

A bell-tossed head sneezed
In a blue daze of incense on
Shrivelled bit lips, then
Just to stay awake, prayed
Too loud for the man to be at rest . . .

O now where has he got to
But climbed an apple tree!

OUR FATHERS

A grey cloud of pollution from Power
Chimneys, mill house, laundries, cars.

The drunk ones take to the square
From eating off soiled linen with

Cigarette ash in the cauliflower
Are left over the whole boom-boom night

Like water sitting in a lead pipe
Are only us 'boy men' in a 'club snug'

At this unholy wee hour of
A Calvin Sabbath river-drags the body

-deserted road back to the condemned
Kitchen house in the blind street row

Under a God is a Scotsman in that
He makes use of all even the dead

Drunk on flat stout and watered gin
'Come on on ahead!' sons shout, 'in!'

Steering our fathers home to bed.

AN OLD PERSON IS FOUND DEAD IN THE
   LOW MARKETS

Like peat still lit (if only just)
Emits an ascending blue smoke,
Her herring-bone-backed ghost –
Against the front-parlour glass –
Is now at least at last

Well smoored in us,

Passes, drifts and dreams apart,

So much wind at night
That slams the door on blind heart.

Spider crawlings on the floor
Stitch a soot-lace to the bed.

All is for confounding movement, as
A faulty roof washes the dead.

A STILL SINKING MAN
Not waving but drowning
                  Stevie Smith

'Midnight and all is well
An Irishmon drown-dead in the Clyde!'
On the dole inside of me

Is the all that I am, an old
Hunched back dwarfsized tinker woman
(Pigtails to the floor) – the Muse

As we but drift in and out
All the one door left you:

Whine of dogs come to their time
Tear at each other's flesh
Saved by no safe thought

With no buttons to our Dress Coat
With no pockets in shrouds!
                         Torn
Up twisted lives dance in attend
-ance: 'Fight each your own turn!'

'Here, I am a well-known
Wrestler, I am!'
               'See him
He needs a good scrubbing!'
                        'Who's
Like me since L'ather-arse died?'

Grandiose entrances of that poor
Buggar's Ghost, the Boogie Man

Grown quite monstrous in time's
                       womb:
'This entrance is also an
Exit!' 'Look Da, Frankenstein!'

LONDON AGAIN

This is Cheapside. Merchants of East
End lay down their rugs at

Market stall, light years from 'home':
Great peoples sunk low to the pawns!

Me, the most important, now the least
Redundant in the alley of any ghetto rat

Throbs a salted open freak on the roam
Through wilderness of densities to dawns

Smoggy at the vague marshes at the knark
                                        of light . . .

'Don't shelter him, don't have any
Thing to do with him' is perfectly right.

I who dart, day by day, through lit night
Under wharf sewer with holes in beads
                                        for eyes

Would not give my brother gunman a penny
For fear he'd begin to look for skies

To glut down to slot machines and stir

Reminiscences of sheer
Uncontaminated air . . .

THE DONKEY YEARS
Soldiers are donkeys.

Picasso

A good soldier does not look
Behind him in and out
Of hospital, jail, asylum

Mixing Scotch and pill
Will be lucky if some day he
Wakes to find the boy he'd kill

So much, become the living
Epitaph of every other
Man's half-blind squint

Back down the morning's steep
Crack in the shaving glass
Brow beats you an ugly guilt

From the beginning, hurtled
School books to the ground
Won jungle greenery to hack

Spray or bomb any island
Hardly on the map, forgotten
As the war behind your back

52

Sons find a bore, will stay
(Now that we are past it)
Always with us like the poor

Undetonated yet human grenade
On backstreet seashore waits
What poison in our puppy fat

Can still make me kneel down at
My own mutilated body glad
'Bang! – Bang! Bang! – Bang!!

'Look, I'm dead. I'm dead!'

THE LET HELL GO OF IT

After I helped you tear up
The gangplank from the Law
As I mounted the bus back

Into town, and my old umbrella
Cracked from an ice-storm wind our
'old acquaintanceship', I

Gaped at and prayed to the driver;
'It would be a good idea,' he swore,
'to let friggin go-of-it!'

Yes, day is night out in
This hailstone-skinning sky
As I watch my broken stick

(All spokes) – fly
Down the whimpering street,
Your liner far out into

The bitch Atlantic now:
An elongated neck of the snow
Goose in flight ship-horn

Honk of the cow in heat,
An art-long, ram-rod flicker
Of fingers, then: GONE!

Well then, good, great, I love
You all the more because
You are not here . . .

BRENDAN GONE

Man seasick with drink
Steadying himself against a lamp post
Before he is game to risk: chance
The long street's precipice brink

Like a very fleshy ghost
Doing a St Vitus dance
In night's depth, the disappearing
Act, the deep, death-fearing, lost
Irish bachelor in a New York flat

After money-making years of waste
Blown up with beer false fat
Losing one's boy taste
For life, woman, or
Enemy encounter during war
At night bolts his apartment door

Alone, window-hurtling to the street

A corpse once young and sweet.

TENTH-CENTURY INVASION

Doves beat their wings
Against their breasts

Bloodying their wings
Bloodying their breasts . . .

Bells ring throughout the book
At the bottom of the lough

Gold running over the
Ruined page

Drowned
Emerald and lilac ink

From the song written in
The shaft of the sun

In the moment on the
Margin
Never to be sung.

HURRICANE DEIRDRE
a forewarning

My hands on your belly can tell
The child kick and wrench until

Better not born the blond eye
Blazed blind of man, the boy.

A devastating child squeals
In your womb woman from burning

In the blood sea bodes no
True good cry that

At great speed the king going
Strong and high the sea road

This gold albino will
Eat the spokes out of the wheel.

THE HUNTED LOVERS

In mild as a warm sea
A winter's evening

Day-moons in a rainbow
A star through water

We wait the kick
Of morning light

On a lonely islet
To the green east

The white gold garlic's
Violet white

Silvering
Our interrupted sleep.

GLOSS

Nor truth nor good did they know
But beauty burning away.
They were the dark earth people of old
Restive in the clay.

Deirdre watched Naisi die
And great King Conor of himself said
'Did you ever see a bottomless bucket
In the muck discarded?'

And comradely Dermot was destroyed by Fionn
Because of the beauty of a girl.
Because of the beauty of a girl
The sky went raging on fire

And the sea was pushed out into rage.
They were the dark earth people of old
And Deirdre pitched herself into the sea.
Turn the page. Turn the page.

THE GHOST

Out of bull resentment
Snores to the moon
At black nightfall

By my side a skull
Hunted Dermot down:

In all the land the lack
Of what was whole,

Flight of the great.
Loss of the seed.
Dermot dead.

I wed this rich old man's
Poor bed who lay
With a young boy
In a gold ditch

Glad on a past day
Of straw and dung

With the sing of his tongue
Filled me.

Gone. Gone.

I lie with a small wizened-up
Old oxen-eyed head.

I stare at a boy
Tall from here to the moon
The eyes: gold pennies,
The hair: honey-brown...

Every night at the foot of the bed
He is my own one.

SAINT COLMAN'S SONG FOR FLIGHT
for Nancy and Brigid – flown

Run like rats from the plague in you.
Before death it is no virtue to be dead.
The crannog in the water, anywhere at all sure!
It is no virtue and it is not nature
To wait to writhe into the ground.

Not one in the Bible could see these dead
Packed on top of the other like dung
Not the two Josephs in Egypt
But would not run!

And Christ's blessing follow
(Is it not a blessing to escape storm?)

Pray to old Joseph not a witless man
Who had the brains not to want to die

But when his time came only and at home in bed,
The door shut on the world, that wolf outside
Munching the leper's head . . .

SEED

By the Bath House where North Man
Thinned flesh by flogging leaf
To the burn of steaming wind
Seared petulant body brawn to bone

Borne in the end by time, the thief
Far from Cahon's Tirkane –
Not a German Greek but out of mind
The slimy stone, the moss remain
And here and there in Maghera: the cinder

A small brickhaired boy whose ancestor
Was some sturdy Dane
Cannot yet say 'Da'

Answers back the centuries 'Yes Sir!'

Strays near the Great Wall in witless disdain
Tramps barefoot on the skull of the charred emperor
Darts back up the blind backstreet
The autumn-coloured clouds his bedtime store

Himself the living trophy left
Of all that red gold gore.

AFTER THE STORM

Wrecked white lupins
To sods crack the young
Red boughs still
With gold buds . . .

The pink ash
Of a fire-dead
Cornflower sky
Has no wing left
To ring us a tune

In slime now with
Moss on the stone
Is the cloud over
The face of
The brown moon!

O redwinged blackbird
Without your worm
What do you do
Where do you go
After the storm?

CIRCLING TO LAND

Flying back down
To edges of day

Root–wandering with
Fever, we

Reach outside the womb.

How black it is
Against the ice

Without stars
Without tears . . .

A long stretch
Of after this

Our sad shelters
Hungering by the shore!

I wish my troubles were
This zooming like a hare

On past out
Of the rat

In the burrow thought

Is a rotten sailor when
It comes down to

A spoonful of love
Would do

Splinters of children.

TWO SOLITUDES
The salmon leaping in our breast
Is the one breast.

John Marshall

You are baking bread.
I am making a poem.

We glow with silence like the full moon.

We are both obliged to wait then
For the ring of cindering bone . . .

You are baking bread until it sings.
I am baking clay until it glazes.

Time is an oven –

You for your moth-coloured grain to golden
Me for my glass pages.

BURNT ORANGE
for Nancy

We drift in sight of mountain ash
Along the high sea wall, down.
Evening hangs on a wash of coral,
A run-up under dead seaweed
To salt rot to wean new seed on.

A boy, knee-deep in foam,
Splashes against your gaze
The malt light of a swimming sun
Strong as shadowing as bronze autumn.

Chestnut from settings,
As dying swans, as smoke, we wait
Hovering, frozen, tearless at the root
With me as mute as you, early as late
Yearning for spring stir:

A blood-bloom from charring
A fire-blackened heather
A throat-blown glass blossoming
Red star upon star:

The light-crazed hazel stain that
Your harvesting eyes are.

STORM AT SEA

Twice this threatening morning
A stranger stood
In your eyes murderously
Deflecting
Each one half from the other.

Would that home could be reached
(Howsoever far!)
That the great clot of wind
Sore with black cloud
Could be leeched
Dry of black blood!

Behind us the fierce glower of dark water.
Before us jigging deckwood.

The mountain wave
Lifts a slanting black wall
Darkening our little boat.

Our little boat is too small.

THE POET AND THE NIGHT

Sleet wind rattles the telegraph
Wires in winter to spring wet.

Debussy, if dying, is not dead yet
Gives himself and us a cloud-bath!

The poet, trying to, does forget
On land, the bombs, at sea, the mines

And in his own body

Cancer of the intestines.

ORANGE MAN
for Norman Dugdale

The sparrow and the bluetit eating
Greased potato skins are chased

By the blackbird. He's chased by
His own brown mate. She's chased

By a shell-in-beak stone-banging
Puffed-out Norwegian thrush that

A gang of tough-looking starlings
Easily chases until a shrewd-eyed

Navy blue jackdaw, the brute size
Of a graveyard raven, invades

The territory that the tiny orange
-breasted robin only thinks is all

His own garden, just can't get let
To stay that dead lonely in.

AGAINST ONCOMING CIVIL WAR

Salmon silvering grey to die
The summers of the past day

Trapped in our own shallow chill
Shadows, then slowly a whole season's

Twilight bleeds like a blue blood's at
The least scathing, opens out

The silk cloud's spider-fingering pine
Against the going away to sea sky

Cannot be wrenched back nor hoarded
But given only as the black ever

-greens go on living high up over
The mountain hill wall, high up over

This little mill town, the mornings
Growing darker than sundown.

MORE TERRORISTS

The prayer book is putting on fat
With *in memoriam* cards.

The dead steal back
Like snails on the draining board

Caught after dark
Out of their shells.

Their very
Outnumbering, swarmy cunning
Betters

My 'cut head' and
Scares me as
Pascal was

At too many stars.

FIRST MOVEMENT

Low clouds, yellow in a mist wind,
Sift on far-off Ards
Drift hazily . . .

I was born on such a morning
Smelling of the Bone Yards

The smoking chimneys over the slate roof tops
The wayward storm birds

And to the east where morning is, the sea
And to the west where evening is, the sea

Threatening with danger

And it would always darken suddenly.

A CHILD OF HATRED

'Well dosed with laudanum, had
To waken 'im to feed 'im!' I am

A 'good child' sleeping on his own
Ill as a drunkard the day after

Needs a taste of the creature
                                    bit him
And when I waken I pray hard

That I may be glad to be still
Alive, if only just, and pray

For all of the people
                          I wake up at
                                          four
Or five and love/hate a more

Than twin brother me in us
But before I pray I forgive

Me to forgive another
And forgive our 'good' even.

That is the way that I live.
That is the way that I take
                              cover

From flesh, world, demon, bone
And the worm, and the child, my

Father and mother the first day
Of summer that does not come.

THE FALL
I cling
to my sinewy
roots
are frail
I fall
    John Marshall

I grind teeth in my sleep.
I have worms, not light
Filtering through
Flowerpot blooms.

An energy of hatred storms
Coursing through the blood is
What wakens me in the mornings.
It's vengeance I want
But vengeance on whom?

The browbeaten child
Eroding on the floor-stone
With roads that end
At the first signposts
Run wild with dogs?

The head hanging down
To the knees is

A stone womb he tries
To hold up by the 'lugs':

'Quit screnchin!
Quit working at yerself!
Quit frownin!
Is yer head hurtin-you?'

'My head had holes inside of it.
I had a fall, I'll
Just have-til thole!
My head has holes inside of it
From being born at all.'

VENGEANCE

I am a child of the poor.

For me there will have to be

Tinfoil: the pink light
-ning pale aquamarine
Morning sea-splashed

Soil dream against

The grave night gale.

HAEMORRHAGE
I bleed by the black stream
For my torn bough.

James Joyce

Entries patent leather with sleet
Mirror gas and neon light...
A boy with a husky voice picks a fight
And kicks a tin down home in pain

To tram rattle and ship horn
In a fog from where fevers come
In at an East Wind's
Icy burst of black rain...

Here I was good and got and born

Cold, lost, not predictable
Poor, bare, crossed in grain
With a shudder no one can still

In the damp down by the half-dried river
Slimy at night on the mud flats in
The moonlight gets an un
-earthly white Belfast man.

EAST STREET

Like a young child bunged
Up with catarrh, cooing
A little teething song,
                            bells, gulls,
The quiet, muffled gong
Of, as if from afar
Off, thunder of pigeons – bombs

Grind of a barrel organ, bare
Feet, cobbles . . .
'Come away from 'em other gets! You
Have shoes on *your* feet!'

Street hawkers lord it over
Children-rankled quiet in
Piercing sea-mew voices:
'Herring-a-day! Herring-a-day!'

'Any oul' scrap arn?'

'Any oul' rags for delph?'

The screeching gulls in a streaky
Bacon sky
            perch tilted

Along the pub roof drainpipe
Wait with military eyes
For the bin men like
A house of boys
                    wait their 'grub':
A silence of greed
Would waken the dead!

A dark field at the bottom of the pavings
Starred with shard upon shard
Of day-eye or sunny pee-the-bed;
Another world behind the dyke
An endless sea behind the brink of brick

Root-running,
                running,
                            down
Miles and miles below the stones
Under a boot black cloud to a
(Gas lit like moonlight)
Mud puddle and then – boom!
Another blast of pigeons.

BOMBAY ALLEY/AN *ORA PRO NOBIS*

Under the sandy moustache,
                                    a grinning
Victory of silence over
Grandmother's tongue
                        lashes out at
The earth-coloured red hand
On the waistcoat's watchstone,

Himself anchored in
A collarless striped shirt, fornenst
The striped wallpaper,
                            winning
Some war us kids can't understand,

Already has his cap on,
Waiting a crooked word from her to
Dramatise victory by retreat, for
Whenever she sells a pig,
                                she wrecks
The house, and yells
                        'What hell's about
This dasmil dunderin-in? Once I had
A home. Now I live on Shite Street!'
And BANG!
                There goes an empty bottle –

Once was a 'dog's nose' of white rum.

Right then, pray a prayer for us, Orangeman
Who burnt us out, rats and all
And I will eat my curses on you
And let you burn the whole of this
Blind backstreet row

Of what's left of the dog's den
                              we're thrown down
                                        born in:

A cracked tile floor, the rain-eaten
Refuse bins, when all the time
'Nothing changes' as the French say

And ay-yes . . .OK: 'No one wins.'

THE WEARING OF THE BLACK

Black velvet short trousers, the shoes
Black patent leather with crystal buttons!

'Awnie, you have them like the Prince of Wales!'

Mother is playing 'See the Conquering Hero Comes'
And 'The Bluebells of Scotland' on the piano.

'Where, O where has my Highland Laddie gone?'

O he is gone to America for
He is on the bloody run!

Our hostess, a bony white-haired Highland woman
Brings us a cup of tea in a rice-paper thin
Porcelain, so delicate, I fumble and drop it . . .

Now, near half a century after, why
Can I recall that flash of fire on the tile
Floor as I scalded my bare knees when I pray
To care even that this rotting self-dinner

-jacketed hero's grave, tonight, in black cuff

Links, at least has the wit to dress for death.

SON OF A GUN

Woe to the boy for whom the nails, the crown of thorns,
the sponge of gall were the first toy.

François Mauriac

Between the year of the slump and the sell out, I
The third child, am the first born alive . . .

My father is a Free Stater 'Cavan Buck'.
My mother is a Belfast factory worker. Both

Carry guns, and the grandmother with a gun
In her apron, making the Military wipe

Their boots before they rape the house. (These
Civil wars are only ever over on paper!)

Armed police are still raping my dreams
Thump-thud. Thump-thud. I go on nightmaring

Dead father running. There is a bull
In the field. Is Father, am I, running away

From the bull to it? Is this the reason why
I steal

      time, things, places, people?

Barman father, sleeping with a gun under
Your pillow, does the gun help you that much?
                                    I wonder

For the gun has made you all only the one
In of sex with me the two sexed son (or three

Or none?) you bequeathed the gun to
Still cannot make it so. I can

Never become your he-man: shot
Down born as I was, sure, I thought

And thought and thought but blood ran . . .

STANDING WATER (A RAG)

Punting into Nova Scotia
Nineteen and twenty-nine, girl
Mother's delph face *creaks,* cracks . . .
(I'm breaking in two myself at five!)

Goodnight all from the beginning.
Goodbye 'cobblestones' but
A backstreet womb wall won't
Let me climb out over it.

We stare at the brick Hal
-ifax sky. A yellow wolf cold
Sits on the leaden Atlantic:
A new world horizon . . . Old

Morning, you are the night of life:
The Russian Orthodox priest who
Has a beard, is the Bogey Man
Will put me in his bag

Is 'America' the Bury Hole he'll
Put me in if I cry?
On the tiny (it stops tangoing)
'transoceanic motor-ship'

Creaks, I cling hard tight onto
A Belfast flapper's strong
Wrist bone. Her stiff new
Red leather raincoat CREAKS . . .

MORNING DARK

Hail-studded sky at the scrake
Of day thrashes the young leaf.
You can see where seed
Is gone corrected to death . . .

A hardhearted father thick as lard
Wants me to grow up to be hard
And tomorrow cannot be counted on.

I stand at the door far in the back
Breathing in the black: aghast.
I am not my father's son
And my mother is a Tartar.

And over the sea is home.
Over the sea: far
Away in the future

Lost in the past like
Locked in a vice . . .

AN OLD MAN HAS A BAD DREAM

It's over thirty years
since I've become an old man!

Oilill

Will the wound ever close
On the boy of ten
Far out in
The drowning man
Has a deep
Rooted bad dream

Trudging to the tin
Shed for Surplus
Blankets and Cod
Liver Oil knows

Mother will
Never come home
From the Box Factory

And Father, back turned
Head in knees
Dead too, is still

Hanging on the Dole.

OUR FATHER
for my sister Mary Galliani

Our father who art a Belfast night
-pub bouncer had to have
A bodyguard, drilled recruits for
The IRA behind the scullery door in
The black back yard,
                              died
In your sleep, in silence like
The peasant you stayed
Never belonging on Wall Street,
Your patience a vice
Catching as a drug!
                         With no hankering
To fly back 'home', the way that you never
Left lifting your feet out of the dung
Of the fields of that crossroad town between
Leitrim, Longford and Cavan, begot
Such a high-strung, tight-knit man, but
For a drinking fit when you vented your spleen
On heaven 'took your woman'
Hissing between nicotined teeth
Collapsing over the 'Hope Chest'
Demolishing the delph closet . . .

Bull-bellowing out in
That hollowing slum subway
'God damn it Christ, why?
That child belonged to me!'

                              Pray
For us now that you and she
Bed together in your American grave
And at what an unnatural price!
The eaten bread is soon forgotten years
Sweltering in the subway – bought
Under Mike Quill nightshift days
Hungering and agitating for
Civil Rights, a living wage
And still, still the injustices,
The evil thing being
That which crushes us . . .

GOODBYE TO OUR FATHER

Father asleep in Central Park without
A hole to hide in you're dead now but

Not inside. Inside it is still
Old nineteen twenty wirelesses

Jangle glass beads:
                              Ay, you steal back
For the cop to beat you over the head

With the night stick for 'drunk as sin'
Singing the Red Flag again
                              but nobody
Cares: It's not an insult any more.

Things bare teeth back to gums and
                                        skull
Grin to privates.
                   I see your bone-naked
Face scrutinising 'Injustices' still!

Never bother! You have a hole to hide
                              in now:

Hide in the bogpit waste we've made
                              of this place
Ourselves by just running away from it.

ICON
for my brother Peter
serving in the Alps

Unholy mother Ireland banging
on the wall in labour

Each season believed
Ivy and thorn would flower

Fell
    slumped over
The Sewing Machine

'Christ of Almighty' swore
Down through a childhood
                              only
A woman or child could
                        bear
Left each one of us with
A grave grace, dark

Not just the same thing as
Wisdom, that what

A *Terribilita* frowning
Nefertiti brow

Vowed never to
Scratch a grey hair
And now, indeed, did not:

We were born in her

Screams to 'Get Out!'

SOLDIERS

The altar boy marches up the altar steps.
The priest marches down. 'Get up now
And be a soldier!' says the nun
To the woman after giving birth. 'Get up now
And march, march: Be a man!'

And the men are men and the women are men
And the children are men!

Mother carried a knife to work.
It was the thorn to her rose . . .

They say she died with her eyes open
In the French Hospital in New York.
I remember those eyes shining in the dark

Slum hallway the day after
I left the monastery: Eyes that were
A feast of welcome that said 'Yes
I'm glad you didn't stay stuck there!'

'Would you mind if I went to prison
Rather than war?'
'No, for Ireland's men all went to prison!'

At the bottom of a canyon of brick
She cursed and swore
'You never see the sky!'

A lifetime after,
                    just before
I go to sleep at night, I hear
That Anna Magnani voice screaming
Me deaf 'No! No, you're not
To heed the world!' In one swift
Sentence she tells me not to yield
But to *forbear:*
                    'Go to prison but never
Never stop fighting. We are the poor
And the poor have to be "soldiers".

'You're still a soldier, it's only that
You're losing the war

'And all the wars are lost anyway!'

FIRE LIGHT

For that near to the empty sky
How cold and bare attics are

Of a pig-iron morning you
Of the scrubbing-board fist

Born to, did die . . .

The sticks too damp to light
The fire, I use your letters

Only to learn that your mis
-spelt words hiss in the blaze

Like tears won't burn in this
Blood sea we drown in but
Do not die in even when

The trying to, the 'sea change'
Is burning you 'away on there'

The more to smelt us back to
                              -gether

Again
    in this so strange
'So Be It Now' as if

It never really were
Or never will be

Only always is . . .

AT CHRISTIAN PLACE

Glowing with the school-empty screech
Of a flock of heady girls, men

With penny-coloured brief eyes
(Like pearls on the skin of the newborn)

Climb the heavy-with-childhood hull,
Hang on to the anchor-chained walls,

Wave flags over Belfast on fire,
Afraid of the gale-torn posters on

The empty lot hoardings, would whip
The feet from under them:
'Kick King Billy

On the bum' and/or 'Kick
The Pope' (thon Whore of Babylon!).

From pawn to pub from pub to pawn
Kick the kick of the hanging man.

A CHRISTIAN SOLDIER SONG
for my brother Brian

Kings in business suits light torches at

My shrivelled up in worm-grip
Of the old rag and bone man won
Bowler hat myth womb of 'Not

An inch' of 'Ourselves Alone'

Womb small as a mice-dropping black
Beats the skin-tight drum
An imp-thumping whack down

Stretching over his shoulder
The bad soldier looking back

Butcher and bread man in the rain
In funeral march for dead gain

Wear on our shirt sleeves the pain

In the Man on the mountain overlooking
                                    the waste
Who wept for man, the beast of burden

Suffering to come on to Him

Blind, cockhorse riding
Children all, all hiding

But cannot snuggle in the womb.

ENEMIES

At the Gas and Electric Offices
Black boats with white sails
Float down the stairs

Frightening the five-year-old
Wee Protestant girls . . .

'Nuns, nuns,' one of them yells,
'When are yez go'n to git
                              morried?'

A STILL FLOATING CHILD

No child ought be allowed to play
Hide-and-seek in these
                                    'nothing but
Piles of stones'
                        where dogs dug up
The floorboards for rats
                                    and soldiers
'looking guns'
                        uncover the cross
And bones of us, born and/or

Died in these wombstones
                                    until

Let out or woke while still
Alive (as if alive for gall)

And sat up and croaked a bellyfill
Of 'goodbyes'
                        all the way
From childhood:
                        the gun-toting

Monklike cops in fours patrol
My morningside dark night of

The iceberg-tip 'child soul'

Trying to hide its drinking deep

Devil white man or with him sink . . .

THE BLACK AND THE WHITE

Sinking on iron streets, the bin-lid
-shielded, battleship-grey-faced kids

Shinny up the lamp post, cannot tear
Themselves away, refuse to come in

From the dying lost day they douse
With petrol and set the town's holy

Cows on fire, as if the burning bus or car
Could light up their eyes ever, much less
The burning of our own kitchen houses

Coming over the TV screen had held
Any surprises, for really, we
Wallow in this oldtime Western, where
The 'savages' are bad
And lost the war because the white men

Always have to be the Good Guys.

THE BRITISH CONNECTION

In Belfast, Europe, your man
Met the Military come to raid
The house:
        'Over my dead body
Sir,' he said, brandishing
A real-life sword from some
Old half-forgotten war . . .

And youths with real bows and arrows
And coppers and marbles good as bullets
And oldtime thrupenny bits and stones
Screws, bolts, nuts (Belfast confetti),

And kitchen knives, pokers, Guinness tins
And nail-bombs down by the Shore Road

And guns under the harbour wharf
And bullets in the docker's tea tin
And gelignite in the tool shed
And grenades in the scullery larder
And weedkiller and sugar
And acid in the french letter

And sodium chlorate and nitrates
In the suburban garage

In the boot of the car

And guns in the oven grill
And guns in the spinster's shift

And ammunition and more more
Guns in the broken-down rusted
Merry-Go-Round in the Scrap Yard

Almost as many hard-on
Guns as there are union jacks.

ELEGY FOR A 'FENIAN GET'
Patrick Rooney
Aged nine
Shot dead

Clouded with slow moving orange smoke
Swirls over the hill-street, the shop

Where I bought the First Holy Communion
                                        Dress
Is boarded up with wire and around the
                                        back
Of it the altar boy was shot dead
By some trigger-happy cowboy cop

Whose automatic fire penetrated
The walls of the tower flat the young
                                        father

Hid the child in out of a premonition!

O holy Christ, why?
                    'Well, it's like this:
Fenian gets out of hell are spawned in
Filthy Fenian beds by Fenian she-devils
                                        will

Bloody not take the pill!'
                              The other
Little children altogether shouted:

'Rats, pigs (nits make lice!) – Burn 'im
Burn 'im, Burn the scum, Burn the vermin!'

ELEGY IN 'THE HOLY LAND'

Girl with the whooping cough
                                        gliding
Through the wall-tall, caved-in
Cliffs of us being kids
                        (still building
'Dragon Teeth Barricades!')

Hankering after the way, you, rosy
With ear aches
                    hung limp over

Fire-bombed iron now, I
Cannot think how long ago

It was your small unsmiling
                                    self
With a doll's pram, scraping
                                        down through
A childhood still in hell for boys
Who tease
            echoing out of sheep
-ishness our wolf
                    'Hello-Goodbyes'

Forget your name even
                    in
                        this
Black shame on us low
-land Scotch drunks call being alive

O dolly-Eurydice, my dark Ros
-aleen dream
                of bog on bog of bone
-grounded cloud, Ireland, my dear

Dragon seed pod . . .

VICTORY ON SHIP STREET

A bomb-blasted pub!

Another blow struck
For our very own
                    corner
On Devil's Island . . .

Stabbed a thousand
Times by flying glass

Two wee girls in
Hallowe'en dress
                    burnt
To death as witches!

A SLIGHT HITCH
March 1972

We wanted to think it was the quarry
but the pigeons roared with the white
smoke, black smoke, and the ghost

-faced boy-broadcaster
fresh from the scene broke down
into quivering lips and wild

tears (can you imagine, and him
'live' on the TV screen!)

had to be quickly replaced
so that the News could be announced
in the usual cold, acid
and dignified way by the

NORTHERN IRELAND BRITISH
BROADCASTING CORPORATION.

GOODBYE TO BRIGID/AN *AGNUS DEI*

I take you by the hand. Your eyes,
Mirroring the traffic lights,
Are green and orange and red.

The Military lorries by our side
Drown out your child-heart
Thumping tired under the soot

-black thorn trees these
Exhaust-fumed greasy mornings.

My little girl, my Lamb of God,
I'd like to set you free from
Bitch Belfast as we pass the armed

-to-the-back-teeth barracks and
Descend the road into the school
Grounds of broken windows from

A spate of car-bombs, but
Don't forgive me for not.

INTIMATE LETTER 1973

Our Paris part of Belfast has
Decapitated lamp posts now. Our meeting
Place, the Book Shop, is a gaping
Black hole of charred timber.

Remember that night with you, in
-valided in the top room when
They were throwing petrol bombs through
The windows of Catholics, how
My migraine grew to such
A pitch, Brigid said 'Mommy,
I think Daddy is going to burst!'

We all run away from each other's
Particular hell. I didn't
Survive you and her thrown
To the floor when they blew up the Co
-Op at the bottom of the street or Brigid
Waking screaming after this
Or that explosion. Really,
I was the first one to go:

It was I who left you . . .

ENEMY ENCOUNTER

Dumping (left over from the autumn)
Dead leaves, near a culvert
I come on
            a British Army soldier
With a rifle and a radio
Perched hiding. He has red hair.

He is young enough to be my weenie
-bopper daughter's boyfriend.
He is like a lonely little winter robin.

We are that close to each other, I
Can nearly hear his heart beating.

I say something bland to make him grin,
But his glass eyes look past my side
-whiskers down
                    the Shore Road street.
I am an Irish man
                    and he is afraid
That I have come to kill him.

KIDS AT WAR

I

Irish kids sneer and jeer
At, salute with cat
-calls the dead body
Of the young British soldier

Gave up his life to save
The Irish woman and kids
Caught in the Spring
-field Road barracks
About to explode . . .

II

The half-kid British soldier
On Lollipop Duty day
Strolls
Into the sweet shop to buy
The Irish kids ice-lollies
Is shot dead
By an Irish kid
Waiting outside
(The one whose head
He rolled his cap on).

WEE FELLAS

I *The Snatch*

It seemed such a cheap
Stage effect of reality that Death
Hiding in the wings
On a foundry roof
Sniping at soldiers should,
Like a childless woman,
Snatch away
A wee chalk-faced boy
Playing marbles in the mud.

II *Gloria*

Glory be to, so
Much for, salute
All us 'armies of
The people' who
Drag away
A 'backward boy'

The eldest of a large
Family in the Low
Markets, sentenced to
Reform-school gaols

For being mental
For being poor
For being tortured into
Yelling 'Yes/No,
I am an "informer!"'

And crucify him with
Bullets for nails

Up by the Zoo.

INTROIT

It raindrops on the cold
Silver windowpanes
Of evening, starting to stare

With innumerable eyes over
The Military, white
-faced as young girls . . .

'We're all going to be blown
To hell's gates' cries
The Welsh one: 'The bomb is

Going off at the gasworks!'
A sudden ball of orange
Spurts over the black

-board sky of chalk
Houses, and old ladies and
Soldiers shake like flowers

Crying 'Christ!' and 'Fuck!'

TEARS

I   *Unisex*

After the bombing the British soldier
Looks up into the barbwired Irish
Twilight. His unflinching open eyes
Deaden, yet involuntarily flood
With the colour of tea
Drenches his combat jacket sleeve.

Now he is hugging,
Now he is giving
                    his male love
To a screaming fellow being he does
Not know if it is a man or a woman.

II   *Lullaby*

When the ricocheting bullet bites into
The young child wanted to walk
In her mother's high heels to push
The doll's pram, she
Gives out a funny little 'oooh!'

And lets the blood spill
All over her bright new bib . . .

No pallbearers are needed.

The young father is able himself to carry
The immaculate white coffin but
Stains it with a dirty-faced boy's
Fist-smudged tears
                        then suddenly cries
Out like a man being tortured by water.

CHRIST GOODBYE

I

Dandering home from work at mid
-night, they tripped Him up on a ramp,
Asked Him if He were a 'Catholic' . . .

A wee bit soft in the head He was,
The last person in the world you'd want
To hurt:
             His arms and legs, broken,
His genitals roasted with a ship
-yard worker's blow lamp.

II

In all the stories that the Christian Brothers
Tell you of Christ He never screamed
Like this. Surely this is not the way
To show a 'manly bearing'
Screaming for them to PLEASE STOP!
And then, later, like screaming for death!

When they made Him wash the stab
Wounds at the sink, they kept on

Hammering Him with the pick
-axe handle; then they pulled
Christ's trousers down, threatening to
'Cut off His balls!'
                    Poor boy Christ, for when
They finally got round to finishing Him off
By shooting Him in the back of the head

'The poor Fenian fucker was already dead!'

GLASS GRASS

> *Try to*
> *understand that you yourself*
> *are guilty of every atrocity*
> *howsoever far from you*
> *it seems to be happening.*
>
> Günter Eich

The scorched–cloth smell of burnt flesh
From morning, a bomb in one of the parked cars,
The gulls, glinting like ice on asphalt in April,
The sun, in a smog of cheap petrol exhaust
Fumes: All bring on the sinusy migraine.

Trudging against an east wind from the cement
Factory (awful bad for the chist!), I wade
Through broken glass in a yellowing black smoke,
Through steel-smouldering streets. There's
Broken glass in my wedding shoes
(I wore them for luck!).

Crossing the shadow-deflected town that burns,
Crossing the always-takes, never-gives man,
Crossing our bone-sieves, crossing our stunted lives,
Crossing the starlings with football-kicking kids
Who make the telephone cables do a war dance,

Once I sipped at your wanton wonder like wine;
Now everything taken from us is reflected back in
-to this Chinese-lacquered black *aubade*
Like piano music in a French film breaks
Into bits of staccato shooting from an M1.

Ducking flying glass from the workers cleaning
Up afterwards, I take to the middle of Royal Avenue
On my way in gold-rimmed Polaroids to give
A poetry reading in Ballymurphy: clutching at
Ragged editions of my own poems, like clutching at

Strands of grass to hold you up from falling
With the crashing debris down the mountainy ware
-houses and hotels! I promised John Hewitt and Des
Wilson, otherwise I wouldn't venture forth again
Into this too-near-to-the-knuckle disaster . . .

Tired of trying to pretend I am not this frightening
Freak has something in common with the terrorist
Of women and children, I read my poem about
The 'icons and guns' and ask 'Now is
That "sectarian"?'
'We're all "sectarian" here!'

Some honest person replies. In the discussion after
-wards Des Wilson says 'I'm frightened of poets.
I'm frightened of their perceptions!'
He wants me to answer.
'Can you put yourself into the mind
Of the man who kills?'
'No.' I lie to the priest. 'I can't',
But I can, I'm polluted

With the poison of violence, born and bred into it:
I'm dying of those dark looks I get from boy
Soldiers from slits in 'pigs', and I try to rub
The hatred from my eyes but it's deeper than 'looks':
The Black is in my lungs now, and in my poems.

My fellow poets call my poems 'cryptic, crude, dis
-tasteful, brutal, savage, bitter . . .' and I remember
The cobbles, cluttered from broken glass, glittered
Like hailstones melting in the warm May noon, and yet
I can put myself into the mind of the man who is cold:

The rich and reverend doctors who live off the misery
Of the people, like leeches, the fat-faced politicians
Grinning on TV at their own witticisms, that all
I want to do is to lie down and join the other
Grinners, grinning with horror, the skull ones,

The 'ones who died' and who are about to die.
(Here, how did all this happen inside and behind time,
And why so often?) I am on the same anti
-depressant as the backstreet kids and their young mothers!

On the streets again, cluttered with broken glass,
White houses, charred black, dear God! Róisín
Somebody (arrested three times by the British Army
For giving her name in Irish) drives us back
Into black smoke. Is Violet Street on fire?
We cut down across from Brian's Mini Market

Through a Crocus Street maze to the Springfield Road.
The girl I saw on Earlscourt Street does not
Matter in this barracks defence mechanism

Spreading its virgin male cancer cells:
A black dog, erect, a tin in its teeth

Is running between football-kicking kids,
Does not see the face-fallen girl cry
Nor care. A dog has more of an in, in our very
Own *Boys' World* . . . A sudden black snow of
Charred newspapers, a lava of lead pencil leaves . . .

(Oh old ladies behind back-yard walls, emptying slops,
Old age 'prisoners' still picking your steps,
Pray you for us 'bombs' in time-parked cars
By backstreet pubs, about to burst
Into smithereens: 'fragments resulting from blows'.)

The chimneypots flower smoke for teatime now,
And Belfast is a beaten sexless dog, hushed,
Waiting for when or where the next blow
Will fall. Against this black, the white seagulls
Glide in again, like hazy-eyed drunks, star the dark.

MIDNIGHT ASSASSINATION

As he stares back behind the fast
-moving clouds at the large
Moons of childhood's upside down
Night field (all wild day
-eye stars), looking up all
At once from putting the milk
-bottles out, the half-asleep, middle
-aged man is shot
Dead.

Now how many loves
Have we lost – sharp, quick
-silver gulls, glinting in
The dawn-dark sky, like knives?

The dead are lying dead in my gut.

NIGHT OF THE MORNING

Scurrying by our own house
Glancing at ten to twenty years
Like friends, like teeth fallen out . . .

I'm afraid to stroll down the blind
Backstreet I was hand-made
A mad man on. I'm afraid of
The boy (a rifle taller than himself)
Soldier lurking on the doorstep.

In this cockpit when the sun
Shifts light to the other side
I hug the in-between tide
Half-wanting to be clean-done-with
The bad-cess, coming true
Dream-curse-prayer, boom
-eranging back . . .
                              Dear Ireland
One would never dream
What a night this morning has been
Like a black flag so
Delicately hovering over
The threshold of the pit
Like a child outside of our
Little town in time, crying

'Yes/No, this is my tribe,
This is my clan. By these pre
-arranged bones, I live and think,
By this skull on a stick, I am

'Womb-wall-barricaded
Bulldozed-down man.'

THE WRONG ONES
for my brother Rory

The howl of the rain beating on the military tin
Roof is like the tolling of a bell
Tolling for a childhood more
Murdering than murdered.

I rise and stalk across the scarred with storm
-erected daisies, night in the north, grass.

My water-coloured twilit-childhood island
-scape is barricaded with circles of rain-rusted
Orange, coiled to kill, barbed wire.

Behind the corrugated iron walls of the barracks
Dead mother rises again to bang bin-lids
On dark mornings to warn husband and sons
'The Pigs, the Pigs are coming!'

The air is filled with shooting, the sky,
The colour of smoke, wends across the soot
-stained grass, the grey Belfast wind
Is blowing against the unblooming-as-yet wall
-flower mind. I reach my hand out and touch
Two-hundred-years-old iron and chipped brick.

I'll be a 'son of a gun' for ever now.
For ever now I'll never be right. I'm one
Of the Wrong Ones.
                          No one will help
The rubber-bullet-collecting kids.
No one will help the grim
-faced teenaged British soldiers or young
Cops, hating the being hated.
                                    We all
Go down the road now sharp and small
As razor blades . . .
                          I pick my steps across
My backstreet childhood as a soldier would pick
His steps across a little mine-filled field.

DARK NIGHT OF THE MILL HAG

She shrieks like a bird hiccuping

'I was the Chief Bombardier . . .
We fought the Battle of Seaforde Street.
In my day I did my stint.
I organised the Turning Over of the Tram,
Full of them shipyard monkeys
Coming home from holding
The heads of Catholic workers
Down in the water till their lungs burst . . .

'A party of a hundred women or so
Led on by me self!

'Nor did we ask them to get out first!'

(On the landing, an oil lamp in her fist,
Ready to plunge the house on fire!)

'In my day there was nothing but the cream
Of Ireland's men in the IRA!
Nothing now but empty
Skites, knaves, craters
Leading double lives, more faces
On them than the town clock!'

She said she saw a man's head pass by
The second-storey window.

'Och notatall granma
Or else he'd be an awful long
John Silver!'

Then the lamp was hurled
And geranium pot after geranium pot
Before whoever it was could
Find her a bed in the asylum from
Childhood to childhood, in a world
-womb to womb: to womb removed.

RENT BOY
to an Irish poet who asked me
in French if I were a freak

Deprivation had my male
Elixir for a dry, white
Wine to go with your cold
Luncheon meat.
                        I am full
Of hunger. You
Are full of your sold
Self, boot-licking power
Must make you hate
That which you fear –
Christ, an odd man out
Cannot be bought,
Only rented
Like the whore.

CREDO CREDO

You soldiers who make for our holy
Pictures, grinding the glass with your
Rifle butts, kicking and jumping on them

With your hob-nailed boots, we
Are a richer dark than the Military
Machine could impose ever.

We have the ancient, hag-ridden, long
-in-the-tooth Mother, with her ugly
Jewish Child

Hangs in the depths of our dark
Secret being, no rifles can reach
Nor bullets, nor boots:

It was our icons not our guns
You spat on. When you found our guns
You got down on your knees to them

As if our guns were the holy thing . . .
And even should you shoot the swarthy
-faced Mother with her ugly Jewish Child

Who bleeds with the people, she'll win
Because she loses all with the people,
Has lost every war for centuries with us.

THE DITCH OF DAWN
for Gerry McLaughlin

How I admired your bravado
Dandering down the road alone
In the dark yelling, 'I'll see
You again, tomorrow', but

They pump six bullets into you.

Now you are lying in a mud
Puddle of blood, yelling.

'There is no "Goodbye",
No "Safe Home"
In this coffin country where
Your hands are clawed . . .'

How can I tell anyone
I'm born, born lying in
This ditch of a cold Belfast dawn
With the bullet-mangled body of
A dead boy
                and can't
Can't get away?
                        A young
Brit soldier wanders

143

Over to my old
                    donkey honk
Of bitter *Miserere* of
Dereliction on the street:

''What is it mate, what is it?

WHAT'S WRONG?'

INTERNEE

It is not absolutely fair,
It is not absolutely wrong,

And it does not hurt
To be jeered at

When you are hanging
Upside down,

When hanging upside down hurts more.

DIRTY PROTEST
God made man out of the slime of the earth

The far-off neons of Belfast glint like crosses.
I'm lying in, lying in, like my own slime.
My face is at the feet of the Supreme
Victim, the People. The People, men/boys, who,

By miscalculation, when
They blew themselves up to the barbed
Wire of the barracks, were
Such manna from earth, the gulls
On the roof tops, yelped for joy . . .

I grope, but all I can do
Is open my fists wide, then
Shoot them tight back in again.

The social worker, the part-time
Student teacher and/or
University lecturer
Volunteer to help –
Fob me off with words
As the prison GP with Aspro –
But how can *they* tell where it hurts?

My left ball, my right ball,
My bellyhole, my arsehole?

I'm in here for just *being*, and stay

Fixed like the crucified: writhing;
Not able to rest; immobile, yet
Sucked down; yet yanked back up
To wherever you are

Blown up, thrown down born alive.

THE LONG KILL/
A *COMMERATIO PRO DEFUNCTUS*
'So Long!' – a twentieth-century way of saying goodbye

These paving stones used to blind
Childhood a *vin rosé* light,
Be flint-sharp weapons, now sit poised

For the street war in the spring rain,
Could be the reason why
I'm, like, dented in:

An empty stout bottle, a 'dead mon',
Gave his whole dole money away
To the eyeless beggar woman

With the red rims,
Had no lids to shut on a yelping howl,
Burst in the end, made

Potato eyes open and pop –
Perhaps for the first or last time –
A year later in a pub; sufficed

But could not do the grief justice.
Something is still, like lying on ice,
Hammers you back in through

This bomb-broken-open now
Forever (blast it!) window. Oh
The cold, Oh the bitter black cold

Draught from all the killings'd blow
(Grief killing the lust)
The arse off you that

Of arms and men so long I should
Like crow-sing the blood-letting
In: all the way from childhood.

HELL'S KITCHEN
An Autobiographical Fragment

The following is the text of a programme written and presented by Padraic Fiacc on BBC Radio Ulster. It was first broadcast on 1 June 1980, and produced by Paul Muldoon.

1959: The wife and I are in an office of the UN building in New York, looking, like miles down, at the graphic East River, the shuddering grave of call girl and gunman. Kids, naked, used to dive from rotten dock wood piers into the filthy grey water. My wife Nancy's criminologist girlfriend from Austria brings her gold plaits up around her head into a neat, attractive braid. I banter with her. 'No, you can't *make* me talk. I won't talk.' But *she* really is doing the talking. How, the other night, a young Puerto Rican had invaded their apartment and how her mother managed to talk him out of rape.

I was hurled back to 1929. New York hadn't changed very much in three decades. Money, Sex (and/or violence) and Politics, the trinity of its one god, Materialism. How I yearned to climb up the gangplank of our French luxury liner, the *Liberté*, and plough as quickly as we could back over the Atlantic into a (corrupt as it had ever been) Europe! Yes, the last time I saw New York was twenty years ago in 1959, and the first time I saw New York was thirty years before that in 1929.

To a child of five, the city loomed over like gold fangs, the glittering, grinning mornings, the silver penthouses, the yellow chequered taxicabs, the long, widening avenues, the endless, blood-drying sun, a light that dogged your heels and made you feel naked to some half-blind god . . .

I said goodbye to New York, goodbye for ever, at least seven times in thirty years. Dog to heel, I returned ever, but only when I was dragged back. The last time I saw her was because a relative had committed suicide. I live in hope that I'll never see her again. But how can you escape New York? This great vulva, this great port of entry *enters you . . .*

> Roller-skating on the tar,
> Hitching a ride on a passing truck,
> Shooting marbles in the gutter,
>
> When they were building the cream
> Iceberg skyscraper on
> 96th Street, we
> Sailed paper boats in the red
>
> Wet cement down a long, wide
> Curb sidewalk to the drain
> By the bank facing Holy Name.
>
> The red clay smelled of sewers and
> The dead unborn foetus . . .

We had a kind of childhood, or in my own case, boyhood or youth, but this was of such a complex, inexplicable nature. Materialism pushed nature itself out the door, so that it came in the window from the fire escape in the guise of a sex fiend. Like a limp child with an earache from teething, exhausted with the heat, we hung over the fire escapes on 98th Street. At night we slept in the baseball pitches of Central Park, and still there was no air. The sand beneath our bodies was like cement dust. They were always building, building, always drilling...

> Can I forget you ever, Hudson River,
> Tar and oil stained, your pollution
> Shining like a ringworm that is a rain
> -bow?

The smell of baking bread on 101st Street. I'm seven years old, buying onion rolls for Mother. A young girl is exposing herself at the window. I never saw the sun shine for so long. The El Dorado twin towers glinting in the far-off blue heat that anything green becomes in such a red humid morning haze:

> How raw you are today, early years
> Ingrowing, growing in through
> The fracture between
> The body and the mind.

> I don't rightly know what the wound is
> New York, you, me, us?

> Some wounds don't heal
> And when they don't heal, they start
> To weep. They weep a kind of pus...

My formative years were spent in Hell's Kitchen, the then black heart of the worst part of New York, and now my existence from that time stands out in front of me and I always want to pull a knife...

Serving on the altar, a Mass for the dead, I noticed, before the coffin was closed, the undertaker had to put make-up on the blond model gangster's girl who died of cancer without knowing it. (The make-up was the mystery of style, the needful fictionalisation, the need in order to communicate . . .) I overheard that her gangster friend tried to bribe the nuns in the hospital to mercy-kill her.

Truth comes from this city like a lash and far too early:

> With Mae West or Tarzan playing in the 'Rose'
> With Sylvia Sidney crying out men,
> Men, only wanted the one thing
>
> There was this dark too sunny day
> Smelling of Fan-Fan Chewing Gum
> When sex seemed the only
> > trouble then . . .

In this office in the UN building far above the city, twenty years on, I remember . . . No, it's almost thirty years now . . .

> Nineteen thirty-one,
> New York City over on
> The West Side, the glittering Hudson River,
> Top hats, summer dresses,
>
> A childhood of sweetheart faces
> In summer hats like glass plates,
> The sun, shining through
> Transparent green streets
> With pink satin roses, the pink
>
> Sandstone penthouses like wedding
> Cakes in German Town, yes
>
> Clean as gone to heaven, we
> Were such empty children then

154

> That later the tired faces
> Bored with waiting in lines for butter
> Flooded back like sea at night . . .

The only escape seemed the sea, the stars.

As a boy, I had Rimbaud's capacity to transform, say, the Reservoir in Central Park into the raging Atlantic, but with Buck Rogers, The Benson Boys, The Lone Ranger, Flash Gordon, and Jack Armstrong, the All-American Boy, all on the radio, we might have been fated to sit in a circle and show each other our pussy willows and teapots until the west of Ireland janitor's wife screamed that there was a 'school of sodomy' going on among the five-year-olds down in the basement. 'Oute, oute! Oute to hell. Yer early awt it!'

The white wood rot in the back yard where the tree died. There was this kid called Adam who stuck his pen-knife into the bark and flayed the wood. He and we grew up to midnight muggings. We stone-crazed, city kids were bursting into birth through stone like trees or anything green. Half-buried, we were in the furnace of a West Side summer, while under the pavement, the subway womb panted far from the 'fiddler broadcasting seed'.

The Irish immigrant men who ran the city's transport were present-day Saint Brendans whilst they ferried you across the Styx into hell. There were so many lost persons like the taxi driver's wife on the top floor dying of a 'tumour'. There was something limp about her, like a bad-boned child. She sneaked down the stairs one night and wasn't heard of again. The taxi driver had to go on living. What hunger in that seething mass of 'like long blue tulips against the caged-in sea' . . . Bernadette who became a governess on the East Side but who, alas and alack, boiled the nappies in a Kosher Pot. Claude, who disappeared. I tried to find you one day but your Spanish father was crazed, was talking to the canary. You were neither black nor white but both, and that was too much for the Americanos.

Dad fulfilled the American Dream and rose from a Belfast bartender to someone who owned his own grocery stores, one in Harlem and one on Amsterdam Avenue. The blacks paid their bills, but not the Irish, and so, no sooner did he soar to the peaks than he was cut down. He lost all. We were plunged into the pit of poverty. Mother, carrying her last child, had to work in a factory near 14th Street. Blanche, our maid, had to go elsewhere. One day Mother and I were called over to German Town. The cop wouldn't let me in to see. Mother came out white-faced: 'I'm glad they didn't let you go in there.' Blanche committed suicide in a toilet:

> Drowning, I look back on summer.
> I don't know where to look for shame.
> I look back into bits.

I had become, early on, one of the Night Riders, fending off the sex fiends on the way to school in the subway. I studied the persons in the subway:

> Vandal-broken glass faces
> Mirror the unguarded bank
> Of us money-marketed are
> Not human sacrifices any more
> To Wall Street's he-whore
> God, but dovetailing, dissolve
>
> Into a tinned tight sardine
> 'togetherness', our dead
> Silent waiting, train-hooted,
> Shunting, not half-shrieked for . . .

Mother was beginning to die. I watched one night the wind rip the gardenia corsage from her coat and scatter it down the dark street. Even in her withering away she gave off a fragrance . . .

> A stray gardenia corsage
> On the subway entrance's
> Top-step, pin-scraps down
> Gum-chewed tasteless air . . .

In the cinema, at the newsreels, she wept at the bombing of Madrid: the frightened people running every which where had wrenched her back to the civil war in Ireland. The strains of 'La Paloma' as she tangoed with the Italian chap on the boat, a young Belfast flapper of the twenties now wore up to the forties and another world war. She would lose her sons. She would lose all. Her husband plied the streets frantically for a job. She beat her hands against the wall in labour as I, the firstborn, watched and waited. She cursed New York. She cursed the whole of America. It was the end of the thirties. By the end of the thirties the American Dream had become a nightmare of reality . . .

In the forties America still clung desperately to the policy of neutrality and isolation from the European conflict. But I was lucky to study in one of the high schools in New York, in which students fleeing the Nazi oppression were welcomed. They had come to this school in Hell's Kitchen because it taught Latin and the humanities. The school was a somewhat old, dilapidated building. One day reporters from a notorious local tabloid infiltrated as students themselves and took photos of the wall paint peeling. The school was also noted for having an overall majority of blacks. Intimate contact with the blacks gave me a sophistication undreamt of. I wrote a play in French

verse, *Des Arbres morts* – and another play in Latin. Poetry
poured forth, and music, and painting. I sat side by side
with a Chinese student who brought words from the great
ancients of his country: 'All under the sky are the children
of God'. Here, in one school, at my most formative years,
were Africa, Asia, the Middle East, and inpouring Euro-
peans. It was exciting and scintillating, like the last glimpse
of the Hudson River as we climbed the stairs down the
basement entrance to report our presence to a general
teacher; in our case, a Polish lady.

All the terrible truths about Hell's Kitchen were true,
but here was the other side of it, the wonderful wide
scope, grass-rooted in the seemingly dead but not dead
past. I dramatised Hudson's *Green Mansions*, drawing a
jungle scene with green chalk and a blue ghostly Rima, a
kind of South American, female Tarzan. What liberation,
what first-flush flowering! I cut a mother and child out of
plaster of Paris in a cigar box with a wet penknife, and
another one in soap and painted it in pastel. I wrote a tone
poem for the right side of the piano, using only the black
keys. My girlfriend, Monique, who was black and white,
filled in the bass part when she played it. In those days, if
the war seemed far away, the Jewish students from Rome,
Paris, Berlin and Vienna brought it home to us. Refugees
like Rolf Pierre Ferand and Lucien and others were my
link with the culture of Europe. Anybody could step out
of a taxi or car or be noticed browsing in an antique shop
downtown – Rachmaninov, Garbo ... One teacher in
particular took over the uncouth slum adolescent and
transformed him into an incurable aspiring poet. Louis
Stark forbade me to read Yeats any longer. Mother and
I assimilated our Yeats with Christian Brothers' wine at
night.

Dad finally got a job as a subway clerk. I helped him

with fractions and maths until he passed his civil service exams. The subway became his life. He could drink with men from the same part of Ireland as himself, and under the sagacious dominance of Mike Quill, the Irish Catholic/Communist, as he was dubbed, the subway workers developed into one of the strongest unions in New York. But if our days of poverty were nearing something of an easement, the new threat was war. It finally broke with Pearl Harbor. The attempt to black out New York was a failure. We all kept our lights on. I watched younger brothers volunteer for the navy and the youngest one dance on the bed with rage and run away to Philadelphia until he got permission to enlist. I watched fellow students throw their books on the floor and dance on them. Art and studies were thrown out the window . . . The great art galleries on the East Side filled with the treasures of Paris and Rome. I stood with Louis Stark and gaped at a load of Picasso's blue period and Rembrandt's *Old Woman Cutting her Nails.*

Music became, in Verlaine's words, 'first and foremost'. I couldn't get enough of Shostakovich, the other Russians, the central European composers, Dvořák, Janáček, Zoltán Kodály, and the Spanish Albéniz, Enrique Granados and Manuel de Falla. But my health broke. At least I could finish my education in the upstate New York seminary, even if I no longer had a calling to the priesthood. There I was to meet the real honest-to-God American after years of Europeans in New York. But the world of the seminary, like the American world of the fifties, was the world of a chicken coop; whatever frightened the chickens was evil, and I, of course, was a born frightener of chickens, a kind of witless fox . . .

My hatred for America increased to the ratio that I watched my mother wither. One night, with Dad drunk, pounding his forefinger on a treble piano key, I wrenched Mother downtown with an invitation card from Padraic Colum to the New York branch of the Irish Academy of Arts and Letters. Padraic was in a bad state. One of his lecturers had failed to show up. Yes, I said, I knew about painting and would stand in. Mother had never seen this part. I blathered on in French as well as English. James Johnson Sweeney had just finished a talk on the late Paul Klee, who died in 1940. I hit Sweeney with the new -ism in Paris, *sur-naturalisme*, and caused a furore. Padraic went over to Mother.

'Do you know that your son is a genius?'

'Yes.'

'Well, make it hard for him. The eagle builds its nest of stones and bits of cut glass.'

'I don't know how harder,' she snapped back, 'I could make it for him.'

I returned to Belfast in 1946. When I hurried up the gangplank of the Swedish liner, the *Gripsholm*, I knew I'd never see Mother again. I took to the other end of the boat and wouldn't wave goodbye to the Statue of Liberty. I had hoped never to return. What was this dreadful wound New York inflicted on us, or was it simply the twentieth century?

Dad could never face that Mother was ill or dying. When she did die I had to return from Belfast to New York in the fifties. New York had changed. It was now an American city. The president of the United States was a world war general, and in the throes of militaristic paranoia even he was suspect to the witch hunts that went on at that time. Two sorts of individuals threatened the Military Mind – 'perverts' and 'Commies'. The Red was under the bed, and in their eyes, probably with another Red.

I renounced my American citizenship in Belfast in 1948 and had to emigrate back to our father. I watched him one day as he staggered home from the subway. He had a few on him and because he was singing the 'Red Flag' a cop hit him over the head with his night stick. I ran across the avenue and rescued him from the cop.

When I raced up the TWA stairs to the plane in 1956, I had hoped never to see New York again, but in 1958 I had to return with my wife, and in 1959 had to say good-bye to a dying father and dying brother. I didn't look back at New York as I followed after Nancy to our French luxury liner. I haven't looked back since. I'm keeping my fingers crossed.

EDITORS' NOTE

THIS SELECTION OF PADRAIC FIACC'S POETRY contains the versions of his poems which the author regards as definitive. They have been arranged broadly, although not strictly, in chronological order. The unifying principle of most of Fiacc's earlier published collections has been thematic, but the editors felt that, for the present selection, an overview of his work would be best served by an arrangement which reflected both the development and continuity of his poetry.

Because he was writing for nearly thirty years before being published in book form, the printed collections do not always reflect Fiacc's evolution as a poet. Between the early 1940s and 1969, when a selection of his poems was published in *By the Black Stream*, he developed a number of unified unpublished collections. Through time, many of the poems in these were absorbed into new, over-lapping collections. During these years he worked simul-taneously on collections in contrasting styles.

A brief summary of the main groupings of his poetry before 1969 may be useful. The early poems of 'Innisfail Lost', written *c.* 1941, have disappeared, as have most of the poems in the next sequence, a collection originally called 'Brendan Odysseus', and then, as it developed into an exploration of the American Indian experience, changed to 'Red Man'. The first versions of the monastery poems in 'River to God' were completed about 1943, but were constantly refined for the next two decades, as were many of the poems in 'Woe to the Boy', an unpublished collection submitted to the AE Memorial Award in 1957. In the late forties Fiacc began a series of poems set in contemporary Belfast associated with novels he was writing at the time: these blended with poetry written on urban themes in New York in the forties and early fifties. Many of these poems were incorporated into the unpublished collection 'Haemorrhage', which was still incomplete when submitted for the AE Memorial Award, along with 'Woe to the Boy'. In the years after his marriage in 1956 Fiacc developed a sequence based on his childhood in Belfast, 'East Street', which included many of the earlier urban poems, and a series of domestic and love poems, 'The Burning Garden'. During this entire period he was working on lyrics based on Irish mythology, most of which developed from plays written mainly in the fifties and sixties. None of the collections from 'River to God' to 'The Burning Garden' were published, but they are all represented in Fiacc's first published collection, *By the Black Stream*, 1969.

The poems written in the shadow of the civil conflict in Northern Ireland pose fewer editorial problems. However, the collections published since 1973 often incorporate earlier material. Although only hinted at in *By the Black Stream*, much of Fiacc's work from the forties, fifties and sixties dealt with war, urban violence, sectarianism and the legacy of the Troubles in Ireland in the twenties. For example, while 'Der Bomben Poet' was never published until it appeared in *Missa Terribilis* in 1986, it was, in fact, written in 1941 – although the title dates from 1981 – and is the earliest identifiable poem in all Fiacc's published work. 'The other man's wound' belongs to the 'River to

God' sequence (*c.* 1943), but was not published until 1973, when it appeared in *Odour of Blood*.

Strict chronological order has not always been achieved: not all poems could be dated accurately, and the poet himself has an instinctive antipathy to an excessively linear approach. Many poems were evolved over a long period of time, and others remained unpublished for many years. The first version of 'Alive Alive O', 1966, was written in the late forties but took at least ten years to reach its final form. A number of poems were included in several of the unpublished collections. If there was doubt about where to place a poem in this selection, the editors have followed the advice of the author.

The early poems in this selection up to and including 'Jackdaw' were all written before Fiacc's return to Ireland in 1946. This section contains one recognisable group of poems belonging to the 'River to God' sequence, from 'The other man's wound' to 'Leaving the monastery'. 'Red Man country' is a rare survival from the American Indian poems, and 'The spring finder' is one of Fiacc's early explorations of Irish mythology.

A significant development in the poems written after his return to Belfast can be seen in 'A childhood friend', which uses Belfast dialect, and initiates a series of urban poems written in Belfast and New York between 1946 and 1956. These poems often deal with poverty, and one of them, 'The donkey years', refers to the problems faced by American GIs returning to civilian life. A number of poems on Fiacc's childhood in New York, begun at this time, have been added to the 'East Street' sequence.

'Tenth-century invasion' and 'Seed' frame a series of poems based on Irish mythology and history, which were written in the fifties and sixties. The next group of poems, from 'After the storm' to 'More terrorists', are from the domestic poems in 'The Burning Garden', and are followed by the 'East Street' sequence written in the late fifties and sixties. The poems from 'An old man has a bad dream' to 'Fire light' represent the only major dislocation to the chronological order of this selection. Most of them were written initially between 1952 and 1956 when Fiacc lived in New York. They have been placed after the poetry on his childhood in Belfast because the poet and the editors felt that in this case thematic continuity had a higher claim than chronology.

A long section of poems relating to the conflict in Northern Ireland begins with 'At Christian Place' – which actually belongs to the 'East Street' sequence. This poem, 'A Christian soldier song' and 'Enemies', all of which deal with sectarianism, were written before the Troubles erupted in 1969. The last poem in the book, 'The long kill/a *Commeratio pro defunctus*', was begun during the 'East Street' period, but was extensively rewritten during the 1980s.

BOOKS OF POEMS BY PADRAIC FIACC:

By the Black Stream, The Dolmen Press, 1969
Odour of Blood, The Goldsmith Press, 1973 (1983)
Nights in the Bad Place, The Blackstaff Press, 1977
The Selected Padraic Fiacc, The Blackstaff Press, 1979
Missa Terribilis, The Blackstaff Press, 1986
The Wearing of the Black (editor), The Blackstaff Press, 1974

PADRAIC FIACC'S POEMS HAVE APPEARED IN THE
FOLLOWING ANTHOLOGIES:

New Irish Poets (Devin-Adair, 1948), *Ten Irish Poets* (Carcanet
Press, 1974), *Poetry One* (Arts Council of Great Britain,
1976), *Modern Irish Literature* (Irish Humanities, 1979), *Poets
from the North of Ireland* (The Blackstaff Press, 1979, 1990),
Voices of Today (John Murray, 1980), *I Have No Gun But I
Can Spit* (Eyre Methuen, 1981), *The Field Day Anthology of
Irish Writing* (Field Day, 1991), *The Great Book of Ireland*
(Poetry Ireland, 1991), *A Rage for Order: Poetry of the Northern
Ireland Troubles* (The Blackstaff Press, 1992).

INDEX OF TITLES AND FIRST LINES